5TH EDITION

Party Wall Legislation and Procedure

RICS guidance note

RICS BOOKS

Figures 1, 2 and 3 are reproduced from Chynoweth, P. 'A Systematic Approach for Evaluating the Requirements for Service of Party Structure Notice', *Property Management*, Vol 18, Issue 4 reproduced by permission of Emerald Publications which owns the copyright.

Published by RICS Business Services Limited
a wholly owned subsidiary of
The Royal Institution of Chartered Surveyors
under the RICS Books imprint
Surveyor Court
Westwood Business Park
Coventry CV4 8JE
UK

Produced by the Boundaries and Party Wall Working Group of the Royal Institution of Chartered Surveyors.

First published 1982
Second edition 1983
Third edition 1986
Fourth edition 1996
Fifth edition 2002
Reprinted with amends 2002

ISBN 1 8421 907 33

Typeset in Great Britain by Q3 Print Project Management Ltd, Loughborough, UK
Printed in Great Britain by MFK Group, Stevenage, UK

Contents

RICS guidance notes

This is a guidance note. It provides advice to members of the RICS on aspects of the profession. Where procedures are recommended for specific professional tasks, these are intended to embody 'best practice', that is, procedures which in the opinion of the RICS meet a high standard of professional competence.

Members are not required to follow the advice and recommendations contained in the guidance note. They should however note the following points.

When an allegation of professional negligence is made against a surveyor, the court is likely to take account of the contents of any relevant guidance note published by the RICS in deciding whether or not the surveyor has acted with reasonable competence.

In the opinion of the RICS, a member conforming to the practices recommended in this guidance note should have at least a partial defence to an allegation of negligence by virtue of having followed these practices. However, members have the responsibility of deciding when it is appropriate to follow the guidance. If it is followed in an appropriate case, the member will not be exonerated merely because the recommendations were found in a RICS guidance note.

On the other hand, it does not follow that a member will be adjudged negligent if he or she has not followed the practices recommended in the guidance note. It is for each individual surveyor to decide on the appropriate procedure to follow in any professional task. However, where members depart from the practice recommended in the guidance note, they should do so only for good reason. In the event of litigation, the court may require them to explain why they decided not to adopt the recommended practice.

In addition, guidance notes are relevant to professional competence in that each surveyor should be up to date and should have informed him or herself of guidance notes within a reasonable time of their promulgation.

1 Introduction

This guidance note replaces the guidance formerly contained in *Party Wall Legislation and Procedure: A Guidance Note* (Fourth Edition). It provides guidance for members of the RICS who accept instructions in circumstances where the Party Wall etc. Act 1996 ('the Act') may be relevant. It addresses the circumstances in which the Act will apply as well as the procedures to be followed where it does.

It provides guidance on the surveyor's role when acting for a client in the early stages of these procedures and on that of surveyors who are formally appointed to administer the Act's dispute resolution mechanism. It assumes that those accepting instructions and appointments in this context possess the necessary professional competence to do so and it should not be regarded as a substitute for this. It deals only with matters connected with the Act and members are advised that other legal, regulatory and practical considerations may also be relevant in particular instances of construction work close to a boundary.

2 Nature and purpose of the Party Wall etc. Act 1996

2.1 Construction work close to boundaries

Despite its title, the Party Wall etc. Act 1996 is not concerned solely with party walls (defined at 2.5(c)). It regulates the relationship between neighbouring owners in the context of a number of specified types of construction work on, or in close proximity to, the boundary between adjoining properties. This work will often involve a party wall. In many cases, however, it will not.

Members should be particularly mindful of the fact that work undertaken wholly on the land of a single owner may nevertheless be subject to the requirements of the Act. The Act, for example, regulates excavations at particular depths within certain distances of adjoining buildings even where no party wall is present. Furthermore, the Act also regulates work to certain types of structure situated entirely on the land of one of two neighbouring owners, in addition to work affecting party walls.

2.2 Historical context

The relationship between neighbouring owners during construction operations is regulated primarily by common law. In particular, the law of tort limits the extent to which a landowner can undertake construction works which, either directly or indirectly, impinge on adjoining land.

In some cities within England these common law rules have historically been varied in certain respects by the existence of local statutory codes. The most significant of these was the London code whose history can be traced back to a 1667 Act following the Great Fire of London. The code first appeared substantially in its modern form in Part III of the Metropolitan Building Act 1855 and, most recently, in Part VI of the London Building Acts (Amendment) Act 1939.

Although some minor amendments have been made to the wording of this London code, the broad effect of the Act is to extend it to all of England and Wales with effect from 01 July 1997. The only exceptions are Crown properties occupied by the Royal Family and the London Inns of Court. From this date common law rules regulating the rights of neighbouring owners therefore have to be read in the context of the procedural and other requirements contained within the code.

In interpreting the code contained within the 1996 Act members should therefore have regard to the cases decided under the 1939 Act and the earlier enactments containing the London code.

2.3 Effect on common law rights

The purpose of the 1996 Act is to facilitate construction operations in the vicinity of boundaries. It achieves this partly by providing a procedural framework which ensures that neighbouring owners are notified of impending construction works. However, in addition to this the Act also grants rights to property owners which entitle them to interfere with the land and structures belonging to neighbouring owners.

Where these rights are given, the Act, therefore provides statutory authority to perform acts which would otherwise constitute the tort of trespass. Although the courts have rarely approved the validity of work under the code which would permanently deprive a neighbouring owner of their property rights, the Act nevertheless authorizes a number of temporary interferences. The demolition and rebuilding of a party wall, the cutting in of a flashing into a neighbour's wall, and the entry onto a neighbour's land to perform other works regulated by the Act, are all examples of the types of intrusive operation which are authorized in this way.

Although sanctioned by the Act the exercise of these rights is subject to two important safeguards. First, their exercise is subject to a duty of care to the occupiers of neighbouring land. A breach of this duty would therefore result in liability in the tort of negligence. Secondly, the Act provides that the rights should not be exercised in such a way that unnecessary inconvenience is caused to adjoining owners and occupiers.

2.4 Unnecessary inconvenience and the role of the appointed surveyor

The concept of unnecessary inconvenience lies at the heart of the statutory code. It defines the limits within which rights granted by the Act can be exercised. The Act authorises work which may involve physical encroachment onto a neighbour's land or which may produce dust, vibration, noise or some other inconvenience or annoyance.

To the extent that such work causes unnecessary inconvenience it will be unlawful and will be actionable by adjoining owners or occupiers as a breach of statutory duty. To the extent that the work is carried out with reasonable care and without causing unnecessary inconvenience it is lawful and its operation is regulated by the Act. The appointed surveyors are central to this process of regulation.

Where surveyors have been appointed their primary role is to balance the interests of the two appointing parties. Their task is to ensure that the building owner is able to exercise his or her rights under the Act, but only in such a way that unnecessary inconvenience is not caused to adjoining owners and occupiers. They achieve this by defining, in an award, the detail of the work which may be lawfully carried out under the Act and by the subsequent monitoring of operations to ensure compliance with the terms of the award.

The remainder of this note provides members with further detail about the nature of this statutory role and about the requirements of the statutory code.

2.5 Some definitions

Readers should refer to ss. 20–22 of the Act for relevant statutory definitions and interpretation provisions. Attention is drawn, in particular, to the following:

a) The geographical area covered by the Act is England and Wales.
b) An **owner** is defined, in simple terms, as someone with more than a yearly tenancy. There can, therefore, be several 'owners' of one wall: a freeholder, a long leaseholder and an occupying tenant, for example, or someone with an agreement to purchase or lease.
c) A **party wall** has two definitions in s. 20, listed as (a) and (b). It can be either a wall standing on the land of two owners to a greater extent than simply projecting foundations (a); or it can be so much of a wall as separates the buildings of two owners (b). In case (b), you could have a building erected by Mr Jones against which Mr Black had, at some time in the past, constructed a building using Mr Jones's external wall to enclose on. The ownership of the wall remains with Mr Jones, but the wall has become a party wall wherever Mr Black's building is up against it (Figures 1 and 2).
d) A **party structure** can be a party wall or a floor separating parts of a building with separate entrances.
e) A **party fence wall** is a free-standing wall, not part of a building, that stands across the line of junction (Figure 3).
f) The person (or company) who initiates any work on his or her side of a wall is described as the **building owner**. The person on the other side is the **adjoining owner**.
g) **Special foundations** are foundations in which an assemblage of beams or rods is employed for the purpose of distributing any load.

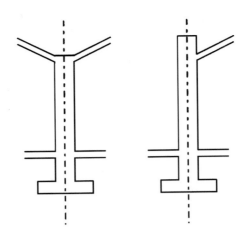

Figure 1: 'Type A' Party Walls

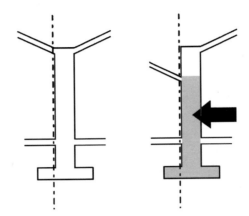

Figure 2: 'Type B' Party Walls

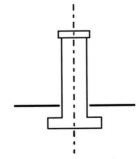

Figure 3: Party Fence Wall

3 Advising clients on the application of the Act

3.1 Surveyors' responsibilities to clients

Surveyors will often be asked to advise whether the Act applies to particular building operations. They should be familiar with the circumstances in which the Act applies and should be able to advise whether service of notices will be required in particular situations.

When advising in this context, surveyors act in the capacity of professional consultants and owe duties to their clients on this basis. This capacity may later change to that of 'appointed surveyor', once notices have been served and a dispute has arisen under the Act (see part 5). At every stage of their involvement with party wall work surveyors should be clear about the capacity in which they are currently acting and to whom their professional duties are owed.

The Act regulates construction operations in three distinct situations. These are line of junction works; works to party walls (and certain other boundary structures); and works involving adjacent excavations. Surveyors should be familiar with each of these.

3.2 Line of junction works

Line of junction works occur in situations where a boundary line (a 'line of junction') is not built on at all, or where the only structure built on it is a free-standing boundary wall which does not straddle the boundary line (see the precise wording in s. 1(1) of the Act). Generally, the mere presence of a fence will not, of itself, mean that the boundary line is 'built on' within the meaning of the Act.

Where these situations apply, a building owner is required to serve a 'line of junction notice' where he or she proposes to build one of the following structures along the line of junction (see definitions in s. 20 of the Act):

- a party wall;
- a party fence wall; or
- a wall on his or her own land up to the line of junction.

Where the building owner wishes to build a party wall or party fence wall astride the boundary line, he or she must serve notice under s. 1(2) and the express consent of the adjoining owner must be obtained. If that consent is not forthcoming, the building owner must build the wall entirely on his or her own land and at his or her own expense but may place projecting footings onto the land of the adjoining owner providing these are not 'special foundations' (see immediately below). In these circumstances, notice is not required under s. 1(5).

Where the building owner wishes to build a wall directly along the line of junction but on his or her own side of it, he or she must serve notice under s. 1(5). In that case, the building owner will again have a right to place footings across the boundary, under the land of the adjoining owner, as long as they are not 'special foundations'.

'Special foundations' are defined in s. 20 of the Act (see paragraph 2.5 above) and will include reinforced concrete foundations. In either of the situations described above the building owner only has the right to place these on the land of an adjoining owner with his or her express consent in writing.

Where a line of junction notice is required, it must be served by the building owner upon any adjoining owner at least one month before the intended start date for the works. Notices should state whether it is intended to lay projecting foundations on the adjoining owner's land and give details of any access requirements.

The provisions of s. 8 of the Act give the building owner a right of access to the adjoining owner's land to carry out works in pursuance of the Act (see part 7).

3.3 Works to party walls (and certain other boundary structures)

Section 2 of the Act grants rights to undertake certain types of work to certain types of boundary structures. The boundary structures involved are generally jointly owned by the building owner and adjoining owner (party walls, party fence walls and party structures). However, in some circumstances, rights are also granted in respect of structures abutting the boundary line, which are situated entirely on adjoining land.

Surveyors should examine the precise wording of s. 2(2) to determine the extent to which the Act applies to the particular structures under consideration. They should not assume that the Act does not apply simply because of the absence of a party wall.

Surveyors should also scrutinize section 2(2) to clarify whether there is a right to undertake the particular type of work which is proposed to the structure. Although there will not be a right to undertake all the stated categories of work to every structure type, the rights granted include the following operations:

- underpinning;
- thickening;
- raising;
- repairing;
- demolishing and rebuilding;
- rebuilding;
- cutting into;
- cutting away/cutting off projections;
- reducing height of; and
- exposing.

Where a building owner wishes to exercise any of the rights in s. 2 he or she must usually first serve a party structure notice on the adjoining owner (see s. 3(3) for the limited circumstances when this is not required). Notice must be served at least two months before the intended start date for the works.

As before, there is no right to place 'special foundations' on the adjoining owner's land without his or her written permission. This would include, for example, a reinforced concrete foundation to a rebuilt party wall, or a new basement retaining wall.

As with line of junction works the building owner has a right of access to the adjoining owner's land to carry out works in pursuance of the Act under s.8 (see part 7).

3.4 Adjacent excavations

The Act does not only regulate works to boundary structures. It also provides protection for buildings where their stability may potentially be threatened by excavations on adjacent land. Before undertaking excavations falling within the scope of the Act, a building owner is required to serve a notice of adjacent excavation on relevant adjoining owners.

The building owner then has a right to undertake certain work on the adjoining owner's land 'to underpin or otherwise strengthen or safeguard' the foundations of adjacent buildings. Indeed, where requested to do so by an adjoining owner the building owner is required to do so, and at his or her own expense.

The following types of excavations fall within the scope of the Act:

- Under s. 6(1), excavations within 3m of a building or structure to a lower level than the bottom of the foundations of such building or structure (Figure 4).
- Under s. 6(2), excavations within 6m of a building or structure that will cut a line drawn downwards at 45° from the bottom of the existing foundation from a point in line with the outside face of such building or structure (Figure 5).

Where required, the building owner must serve the notice of adjacent excavations on any adjoining owner at least one month before the intended start date for the works.

Once again, there is no right to place 'special foundations' on the adjoining owner's land without his or her written permission and the building owner has a right of access to the adjoining owner's land to carry out works in pursuance of the Act under s. 8.

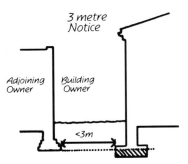

Figure 4

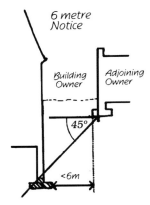

Figure 5

4 Service of notices

4.1 The importance of valid service

Service of primary notices (as required by ss. 1, 3 and 6 of the Act) commences a statutory procedure. Any deficiency in service may render the whole procedure invalid (see part 6). The resulting delay to the project, with consequent increase in costs, may be considerable. Where surveyors are responsible for the preparation and service of notices they should be aware of the professional liability issues in this respect.

It is particularly important to comply with the strict time limits stated in the Act for service of notices. These give adjoining owners adequate time to consider the impact of the proposals and to enable counter-notices, queries and ultimately disputes to be dealt with properly. These time limits may not be overridden other than by agreement between the owners. A building owner must be advised as to the appropriate time required for obtaining statutory consents and serving notices at the outset so that expensive delays can be avoided.

4.2 Content of notices

Any notice should give sufficient detail for the adjoining owner to assess the impact of the proposals on his or her building. Failure to provide this may invalidate the notice. The notices may be accompanied by drawings. In any event, they should always comply with the Act's specific requirements for the particular notice being served. Surveyors should make reference to the Act in this respect.

All notices are required to be served by the owners, although they can authorise their surveyor, acting as their agent, to sign and serve notice on their behalf. Before surveyors serve a notice on behalf of clients they should ensure that they have the necessary written authority to do so. It will often be appropriate to use the form of surveyor's appointment and authority provided in Appendix A to this guidance note, which also deals with the formal appointment of surveyors under the Act.

All notices should:

- be in writing;
- give the name and address of the building owner. If owned in joint names, all joint owners must be named;
- be signed. Signature should be by the owner(s) or a person fully authorised to sign notices on their behalf;

- be dated. The date on the notice should be the date on which it is delivered or posted to the recipient owner or delivered to the adjacent premises;
- be properly served on all adjoining owners as defined by the Act, whether freehold or leasehold. If a property is owned in joint names it is only strictly necessary to serve the notice on one of them (*Crosby* v *Alhambra Co. Ltd* [1906] 1 Ch 295). It is, however, good practice to effect service on all joint owners whose identities and addresses are known;
- state the nature and particulars of the intended works and the date on which it is intended to commence the works. Descriptions of intended works should be directed toward a lay recipient and contain sufficient detail to enable the extent of works to be understood;
- where served under s.6, be accompanied by plans and sections showing the site and depth of any excavation, and the site of any new building, and state whether the building owner intends to underpin or otherwise strengthen or safeguard the foundations of the adjoining owner's foundations;
- where served under s.3 and involving special foundations, be accompanied by drawings showing the special foundation details and reasonable particulars of the loads to be carried.

4.3 Methods of service

Section 15 sets out permissible methods of service of notices and other documents under the Act. It provides that notices may be served on an individual in person or by posting it to his or her usual or last-known residence or place of business in the UK. In the case of a body, corporate service can be effected by delivering it to the secretary or clerk at the registered or principal office or by posting it to the secretary or clerk at that office.

Any notice (or other document) may alternatively be served by addressing it to 'the owner' of the premises (naming them), and delivering it to a person on the premises or, if no person to whom it can be delivered is found there, fixing it to a conspicuous part of the premises.

It is prudent to make best endeavours to ensure the intended recipient becomes aware of the notice and that a time allowance is made for postal delivery of both the notice and an acknowledgement or counter-notice. It is good practice to record the date of postage in an office post book.

4.4 Responses to notices

When notice is received the adjoining owner can do one of three things and his or her choice will, to some extent, determine the proceedings that follow.

4.4.1 The adjoining owner does nothing

- In the case of party structure notices and notices of adjacent excavation, the adjoining owner's failure to respond within 14 days of service of notice will give rise to a deemed dispute. The s. 10 statutory dispute resolution process then commences.
- It may be necessary to serve a request under s. 10(2)(b) on the adjoining owner to appoint a surveyor within ten days, in default of which the building owner can appoint a surveyor on behalf of the adjoining owner. It is not possible, in these circumstances, to appoint an agreed surveyor.
- In the case of line of junction notices served under s. 1(2), if the adjoining owner fails to respond within 14 days the building owner may then build his or her proposed wall entirely on his or her own land and can proceed as soon as the notice period has elapsed. As mentioned in paragraph 3.2 above, he or she may also place projecting footings on the adjoining owner's land providing they are not 'special foundations'.
- In the case of line of junction notices served under s. 1(5), the adjoining owner's failure to respond will allow the building owner to proceed with his or her proposed works after the notice period has elapsed. Again, this will include the right to place projecting footings on the adjoining owner's land providing they are not 'special foundations'.

4.4.2 The adjoining owner agrees to the works as proposed

- The adjoining owner may express his or her consent in writing to the works as proposed in the notices. This should not be considered as a waiver by the adjoining owner of his or her rights under the Act, but simply a statement that, at present, there is nothing in dispute.
- Nevertheless, the granting of unconditional consent to the building owner to undertake the works leaves an adjoining owner with less protection than would be available if consent had not been given. Adjoining owners should therefore be advised of the need to state the terms on which any consent is granted and the desirability of recording the current state of their premises in an agreed schedule of condition.
- Consents should contain an express statement that they are not intended to waive the adjoining owner's rights under the Act and that disputes which subsequently arise in connection with the works are to be resolved in accordance with the s. 10 procedures.

4.4.3 The adjoining owner expresses dissent to the works as proposed

- If the adjoining owner dissents to any notice served then the dispute must be settled in accordance with s. 10 of the Act.

- Each owner may agree to the selection of one surveyor (the agreed surveyor) who will determine the matters in dispute.
- Alternatively, each party appoints their own surveyor. The two surveyors select a third surveyor. Two of the three surveyors then determine the matters in dispute. Either of the surveyors, or either of the owners, may call upon the third surveyor to determine matters on which they cannot agree (see part 9).
- Section 10 allows the surveyors to determine any matters connected with any work to which the Act relates and which are in dispute. These include the right to execute the work, the time and manner of execution of the works and any other matter arising out of or incidental to the dispute.

4.5 Service of counter-notices

Following receipt of a notice for works under s. 2 of the Act, the adjoining owner may serve a counter-notice within one month, setting out such additional works to the party structure or to special foundations as they may reasonably be required. This must include plans, sections and particulars of that work.

The building owner must comply with the request unless to do so would be injurious, cause unnecessary inconvenience or cause unnecessary delay to the works. The costs of the work will be apportioned according to the benefit to either party.

5 Accepting appointments under the Act

5.1 Letters of appointment

The appointment of a surveyor arises out of a dispute between the two owners, following service of notice. A dispute arises when there is an express dissent to a notice or when a party structure notice or notice of adjacent excavation is not responded to by the adjoining owner within 14 days.

In either of these situations the parties must then appoint surveyors as described in paragraph 4.4.3 above. Appointments must be made in writing and be personal to the surveyor appointed rather than being made in the name of his or her firm. (See the surveyor's appointment and authority in Appendix A for an appropriate form of appointment.)

An appointment must be signed by the owner of the relevant property or by an agent specifically authorised in writing to make such appointment. In the latter case it is good practice to request a copy of the agent's authority. Where property is held in joint ownership, for example, a house owned by both a husband and wife, the appointment must be signed by all relevant parties.

If an appointment is invalid then a subsequent award will also be invalid (see part 6). It is, therefore, good practice for the appointed surveyors to provide each other with copies of their written appointment before proceeding with any work to negotiate an award.

The selection of a third surveyor should be made by exchange of letters between the surveyors and it is not necessary for a letter of appointment to be sent to the third surveyor at this stage. It is good practice to select a third surveyor with a sound knowledge of the Act and with extensive experience of administering its provisions.

5.2 Who may act as surveyor?

Nobody who is a party to a dispute may be appointed as a surveyor in that dispute. Parties may not, therefore, act as their own surveyor. Apart from this, there are no statutory restrictions on who may be appointed as a surveyor under the Act.

Despite this, persons accepting appointments should satisfy themselves that they are able to administer the statutory requirements fairly and independently. Before accepting such appointments surveyors should therefore consider whether there is a potential conflict of interest which could prevent this (see paragraph 5.5 below).

5.3 Status of party-appointed surveyors

Surveyors appointed under s. 10 of the Act undertake a statutory role. The appointed surveyors should seek to conclude an award that fairly sets out the rights and obligations of both owners, ensuring that the work specified in the award is permissible under the Act. The award should enable the building owner to carry out the work in such a way that unnecessary inconvenience is not caused to adjoining owners or occupiers.

An appointed surveyor cannot be discharged by either appointing owner. The appointment only comes to an end if the surveyor dies or declares him or herself incapable of acting. This ensures that the surveyor is able to conclude an award without undue interference from their appointing owner.

The appointed surveyor should seek to identify and represent the interests of their appointing owner but this should not extend to following instructions from their appointing owner where these conflict with their duties under the Act.

The appointed surveyors should act diligently in considering information provided to them and in seeking to reach agreement and conclude an award. The Act allows one surveyor to conclude an award alone if the other surveyor has refused to act effectively or has neglected to do so for ten days after being so requested.

5.4 Appointment as agreed surveyor

The two owners may concur in the appointment of an 'agreed surveyor'. That surveyor must act impartially and work towards concluding an award that is fair to both owners, regardless of which owner made the initial appointment or whether one owner is an established client.

The agreed surveyor must conclude an award that sets out the rights and duties of both parties and the works to be carried out.

If an agreed surveyor refuses to act or neglects to do so for a period of ten days after being required to act by either party, then his or her appointment will end. Both owners must appoint another agreed surveyor or individual surveyors who will then settle the dispute.

5.5 Professional conduct issues

Surveyors must appreciate that the role of appointed surveyor differs significantly from their role in providing advice on the application of the Act or in serving notices on a client's behalf. Once appointed under the Act surveyors perform a statutory function. They are no longer solely responsible to their client but will owe duties to both parties to the dispute (see part 6). To emphasise this, it is customary for surveyors to refer to the party who appoints them as their 'appointing owner' rather than their client.

A surveyor engaged on the supervision of works which themselves trigger the requirement for service of notice may not be best placed to accept an appointment as the building owner's surveyor. Surveyors should satisfy themselves that no conflict of interest arises in these or other circumstances before accepting appointment.

Particular difficulties may arise where a surveyor considers accepting an appointment as agreed surveyor. In practice there may be a perceived conflict of interest if a candidate for agreed surveyor had previously acted as the building owner's agent. Surveyors should not accept appointments in these situations without having first drawn the potential conflict of interest to the attention of both parties and having received their written confirmation that they have no objection to this. However, there may well be circumstances in which professional judgment dictates that it would be prudent to decline to act.

6 Powers and duties of appointed surveyors

6.1 Statutory purpose of surveyors' role

Once appointed, either the agreed surveyor acting alone, or the three surveyors (two party-appointed surveyors and the third surveyor) acting collectively, constitute what has been referred to as a 'practical tribunal' (*Adams* v *Marylebone Borough Council* [1907] 2 KB 822).

The practical tribunal's role differs from that of most conventional tribunals (for example, the courts and arbitrators). It is charged with the specific task of enabling the building owner to exercise his or her rights under the Act in such a way that unnecessary inconvenience is not caused to adjoining owners or adjoining occupiers. It does this by regulating the nature and conduct of the construction operations even-handedly between the parties.

Because the surveyors act as members of a tribunal their actions are restricted. They must ensure that they act within their proper jurisdiction and that they only exercise powers which have been granted to them by the statute. Where surveyors exceed either their jurisdiction or their statutory powers their awards will be invalid and may be set aside by the courts. The surveyors are also subject to legal duties, both individually, and as members of the tribunal.

6.2 Surveyors' duties

The tribunal is under a duty to act impartially between the parties. It also owes a duty to perform its duties diligently and to exercise reasonable care in so doing. Where the tribunal's functions are exercised by a single surveyor (either an agreed surveyor or a third surveyor) all these duties are owed by the surveyor in a personal capacity.

Where surveyors act as party-appointed surveyors they owe a duty of care to their own appointing owner. They will, however, continue to owe a duty to both parties to perform their duties diligently. Hence, whilst safeguarding the interests of their own appointing owner within the tribunal, surveyors should not follow instructions from that owner where this would frustrate the proper function of the legislation.

Where the tribunal's functions are being exercised by the two party-appointed surveyors, its duty of impartiality is discharged because each party has its own voice on the tribunal, in the form of their own surveyor. In these circumstances, whilst the surveyors must exercise professional independence and integrity, they are probably not subject to a legal duty to behave impartially (*Chartered Society of Physiotherapy* v *Simmonds Church Smiles* [1995] 1 EGLR 155).

6.3 Surveyors' jurisdiction

The surveyors will only have jurisdiction if the tribunal, of which they form a part, has been properly constituted. They will also only have jurisdiction to address matters within their competence.

6.3.1 Proper constitution of the surveyors' tribunal

The Act sets out detailed requirements for the composition of the surveyors' tribunal and for the appointment of the surveyors themselves (see ss. 10(1)–(9)) as well as for the service of notices. These requirements have already been discussed in parts 4 and 5 of this guidance note.

Where there has been a failure to follow them precisely, the surveyors will lack jurisdiction and the courts will readily declare their awards to be invalid. Because the Act sanctions the interference with the property rights of adjoining owners, the courts require the Act's requirements to be followed scrupulously and have advised that 'the approach of surveyors to those requirements ought not to be casual' (*Gyle-Thompson* v *Wall Street (Properties) Ltd* [1974] 1 All ER 295).

6.3.2 Competence of the surveyors' tribunal

Section 10(10) of the Act provides that the surveyors are only competent to make awards on matters which are in dispute between the parties and which are also connected with work to which the Act relates.

The nature of 'disputes' within the meaning of the Act has been explored in paragraph 4.4 of this guidance note and there will rarely be any doubt as to whether matters are in dispute. The necessary degree of connection between the dispute and work to which the Act relates often causes more difficulty.

Although appointed surveyors are frequently called upon to resolve a variety of disputes between the parties they must be careful to distinguish between those that must be settled by consensual negotiation and those that can properly be addressed by their award. Disputes about crane oversailing, easements, and the general conduct of piling operations outside the prescribed distances, are all examples from the first of these categories and the surveyors have no jurisdiction to address them in an award.

6.4 Surveyors' powers

Where the surveyors have jurisdiction under the Act, they have power under s. 10(12) to make binding awards which may determine any of the following issues:

- the right to execute work under the Act;
- the time and manner of executing any such work; or
- any other matter incidental to the dispute referred to them, including the costs of making the award.

An award which purports to determine some other issue, or which determines one of these issues in a manner which was not contemplated by the Act, will have exceeded the statutory powers (*ultra vires*) and will be invalid.

The surveyors' power to determine the right to execute work is, in reality, only a right to declare the existence of a particular statutory right in a particular situation. The surveyors have no power to confer new rights on the parties.

The power to determine the time and manner of execution of work is central to the surveyors' role. The courts will not interfere in surveyors' awards where they restrict themselves to the exercise of this power.

Surveyors should, however, be extremely cautious about assuming the existence of powers to deal with matters which are in some way 'incidental to the dispute referred to them'. Surveyors have an express power, under this heading, to adjudicate on the professional costs of making the award, and also have the power to implement the statutory rules on compensation, making good, and on the liability for the costs of the work. It is unlikely that they have any further powers.

6.5 Enforcement of surveyors' awards

A valid award creates legal obligations between the parties. A breach of the terms of the award, therefore, creates a legal liability, which can form the basis for court action by an aggrieved party. A successful action in the courts would result in a court judgment, which could then be enforced against the defaulting party in the normal way.

There have also been occasions where county courts have treated surveyors' awards as arbitration awards and have granted leave to enforce them directly as court judgments, under s. 66 of the Arbitration Act 1996. Where this procedure is available, this removes the need to obtain a court judgment before taking enforcement action. The legality of this procedure is open to question. Surveyors should therefore always recommend that clients obtain legal advice before relying on it as a valid means of enforcement.

7 Surveyors' role in preparing primary award

7.1 Preparing schedules of condition

In most cases an award should include a schedule of condition of the adjoining owner's building. Schedules should be compiled before any building works start and should include those parts of the adjoining building and grounds that may be affected by the works. The extent of the schedule depends on the nature and location of the proposed works. For example, where it is proposed to build higher than the adjacent building, roofs should be closely examined as they could be damaged by falling debris or materials.

It is particularly important to record cracks and their width and location. It is often useful to include a simple drawing, as photographs do not always show minor defects. Ultimately, the purpose of the schedule is to identify to what extent any claim for damage is a valid one and, if it is, the extent of the damage. The schedule should be sufficient to avoid leaving significant areas of doubt and this will be a matter for the judgment of the two surveyors.

It is usual for the building owner's surveyor to prepare the schedule of condition which has to be checked and agreed by the adjoining owner's surveyor.

A sample form of a schedule of condition is shown in Appendix B.

7.2 Agreeing the contents of the award

The building owner's surveyor will usually prepare a draft award and send it to the adjoining owner's surveyor for comments. Whilst there is no prescribed award format, it is recommended that surveyors use the form suggested in Appendix A. An award will usually include relevant drawings of the notifiable works, method statements, a schedule of condition and any limitations on the time and manner of carrying out the work.

The surveyors agree the working conditions, such as the hours for noisy works, whether weekend working is acceptable, protection required to any exposed party walls, security arrangements and fees to be paid and by whom. Method statements may be attached for particular operations such as demolition or details of access onto the adjoining owner's land.

7.3 Provision for disturbance, making good and compensation

Awards should make express provision for the making good of damage caused by relevant works under s. 2(2) of the Act and, where appropriate, for the payment of compensation for damage caused by the stated works under s. 1. Surveyors should make reference to the Act to determine the precise situations in which such compensation and making good are applicable.

More generally, s. 7(2) also requires the building owner to pay compensation for loss or damage caused by any works executed in pursuance of the Act. For example, if car parking is impeded because of scaffolding, it may be justifiable for the building owner to pay the cost of providing parking elsewhere.

Where such loss or damage can be anticipated in advance of the work, provision should be made for payment within the award. Note that such compensation is only available for justifiable and calculable losses and not for mere inconvenience. See also paragraph 8.4 below.

Where a building is laid open under s. 2(2)(e) the surveyors should also consider whether it is appropriate for adjoining owners and occupiers to receive a payment in respect of inconvenience and disturbance under s. 11(6). If so, a fair allowance should be assessed for this in advance of the work and included in the award provisions.

7.4 Costs of the work (expenses)

The Act sets out various guidelines on the responsibility of the owners for the costs of works.

In most cases the costs of works under this Act shall be defrayed by the building owner. This is because the building owner will benefit from the works which he or she has organized, and the adjoining owner does not usually benefit from them.

Exceptions to this rule include cases where building works are required because party structures (for which there is a joint liability) are defective. The costs of remedial works, and the proportion of fees that relate to them, should be appropriately split between the owners who will benefit from the works unless it can be shown that one owner is responsible for the defect.

Where the building owner carries out works to improve his or her property and lays open the adjoining owner's premise, 'a fair allowance' is to be paid for disturbance and inconvenience suffered by the adjoining owner.

When a building owner carries out improvements or extensions to his or her property at personal cost and the adjoining owner subsequently makes use of those works, the adjoining owner may have a liability to make a payment to the building owner (or his or her successor in title). This is calculated as a fair proportion of the costs and expense of the relevant portion of the original works, at present day value.

Where damage is caused to the adjoining owner's property the adjoining owner has the right to a financial sum covering the costs for remedial works as opposed to having the works executed.

Where a building owner proposes to reduce the height of a party wall or party fence wall (to no less than 2m high) the adjoining owner can serve a counter-notice requesting the existing height of the wall to be maintained. If so, the adjoining owner has to pay a due proportion of the cost of retaining that wall including the full cost of its subsequent maintenance to the extent that it exceeds that which is necessary for the purposes of the building owner.

7.5 Costs of the award (surveyors' fees)

Responsibility for the fees of the appointed surveyors is determined by the surveyors (to the extent that these have been properly incurred in administering the Act's provisions). Responsibility usually follows the apportionment of costs for the works. Fees for both are, therefore, usually paid by the building owner. Where the costs are defrayed by both owners, the fees of each surveyor may be apportioned accordingly, or each owner may pay their own surveyor's fees.

It is usual for the award to include the fees of the surveyor appointed by the adjoining owner as a lump sum based on time incurred, including an allowance for subsequent inspections, and an hourly rate should further involvement become necessary through change of design, problems found on site, or damage. Only fees which are proportionate to the tasks involved should be included in the award in this context. The surveyor appointed by the building owner would normally agree his or her own fees with the building owner.

7.6 Signature and service of awards

Once an award has been agreed it should be signed by the agreed surveyor, by two of the three surveyors, or by the third surveyor, as appropriate. Section 10(14) of the Act states 'where the surveyors appointed by the parties make an award the surveyors shall serve it forthwith on the parties'.

The award must be sent to the owners or an authorised agent, or it will not be valid.

The owners should be advised of their right to appeal the award within 14 days if they believe that it has been made improperly.

7.7 Entry onto adjoining land

Section 8 gives the building owner, his or her servants, agents and workmen the right to enter the premises of the adjoining owner for the purpose of executing any work in pursuance of the Act. Access is only available during usual working hours.

Details of access should be determined by the appointed surveyors when agreeing an award, and should include such restrictions and safeguards as are necessary to protect the adjoining owner.

Notice must be served upon any adjoining owner and occupier at least 14 days in advance. In case of emergency there is only a need to serve such notice as may be reasonably practicable. This may mean a need to serve a notice for access on an occupier who is not an owner as defined by the Act.

Preventing access is a criminal offence. If access is not available, then the building owner may break in if accompanied by a police officer.

It is generally accepted that there is a right to erect scaffolding to facilitate the access, if reasonably necessary.

Any appointed surveyor may have access to the land of the building owner or adjoining owner to carry out their role, subject to notice as above.

7.8 Security for expenses

The Act makes provision for both the building owner and adjoining owner to provide security for expenses for which they may become responsible under the Act. The provision of security will only be appropriate where there is a particular risk of default in payment of such expenses, such as the potential liability arising out of the non-completion of the work, the financial standing of the relevant owner, or from inevitable and foreseeable damage which may be caused by it. The risk of default, justifying payment of security, should be assessed in each case.

If the adjoining owner wishes to serve notice requiring the building owner to provide him or her with security, this must be done before work commences. If the parties cannot agree the amount of the security then this will be determined by the surveyors. The arrangements for payment of security should, in any event, be described in the award.

Where an adjoining owner has required the building owner to carry out additional works, for example under s. 4 of the Act, the building owner can request security from the adjoining owner. If this is not paid within one month of the request, or within one month of an award determining the security, the building owner is not obliged to comply with the counter-notice. As with security required by an adjoining owner, all arrangements should be described in the award.

8 Surveyors' role subsequent to publication of primary award

8.1 Interim and final inspections

Within their award the appointed surveyors may include a provision for subsequent inspections to ensure that the terms of the award are being complied with or to inspect any detail or structure opened up during the works.

It is usual to provide for adequate interim inspections and for a final inspection to recheck the schedule of condition.

8.2 Design changes

Where there are changes to the design of works included in the award these must either be agreed by the parties, as anticipated by s. 7(5) of the Act, or, in the event of disagreement between them, referred to the surveyors to be determined by a further award (an 'addendum award').

Surveyors can obtain their appointing owners' authority to agree such changes on their behalf. Where the surveyors are able to reach agreement this is then recorded in an exchange of letters between them. In these circumstances there is no requirement for an addendum award, even for extensive changes in design.

8.3 Where additional work becomes necessary

Subsequent to the service of a notice, the building owner may wish to undertake additional work under the Act, which was not referred to in the original notice.

Where this work is closely related to the work described in the original notice it may legitimately be considered as a design change and dealt with according to the procedures described in the previous paragraph. In cases of doubt the surveyors should consult with their appointing owners to confirm that they are in agreement with matters being dealt with in this way.

Where the additional work is entirely unrelated to that proposed by the original notice the building owner will only be permitted to undertake it in accordance with the Act's requirements. In an extreme situation, in the absence of consent by an obstructive adjoining owner, there may be no alternative to serving a new notice on the adjoining owner and starting the statutory procedure afresh. As this will result in delay and additional expense it will not normally be the most appropriate course of action.

It is preferable for the surveyors to resolve the issue consensually. Assuming that they have their appointing owners' authority to do so they may achieve this by reaching agreement to the additional works on their behalf without the requirement for service of a further notice. This reflects the inherent right of parties to agree to works under the Act without service of notice which is expressly stated, in the case of s. 2 works, in s. 3(3)(a).

Providing surveyors obtain all adequate additional authorities, they can expedite the procedure by receiving the notice, consenting to the works and waiving the statutory notice period for commencement of the works, on their appointing owner's behalf.

8.4 Awarding compensation and making good

The surveyors should require the building owner to make good damage caused by the works where this is appropriate under the Act. Express provision will usually have been made for this in the primary award (see paragraph 7.3).

The adjoining owner can instead require the surveyors to determine the cost of the making good and this sum must then be paid to him or her in lieu of making good. Where damage is caused by works under s. 1 the Act provides for the payment of compensation rather than making good. Surveyors should, therefore, require the building owner to pay compensation for such damage unless both parties have expressly consented to him or her making good.

As well as addressing damage to the adjoining owner's property in this way the surveyors may also require the building owner to pay compensation for certain non-physical losses or damage caused by the works. Surveyors should refer to s. 7(2) in this respect. For compensation to be payable in these circumstances the adjoining owner must have experienced an actual loss or damage rather than simply an inconvenience. The loss must also be capable of quantification by the surveyors.

8.5 Changes of ownership

The Act is relatively unclear on the procedures that apply when ownership changes.

Where the building owner changes the procedure must start afresh as the building owner who intends to carry out the work must be the one who served notice. In addition, the adjoining owner's response to the initial notice is likely to have been influenced partly by the identity and intent of the building owner at the time.

If the adjoining owner changes, common practice has been that the appointment of the adjoining owner's surveyor continues and that the rights and duties of the adjoining owner pass to the new adjoining owner. This avoids unnecessary delay, cost and inconvenience to the building owner by virtue of a change of adjoining owner. It also prevents an adjoining owner thwarting a building owner's intention to proceed with work by, for example, transferring ownership of the adjoining property to a subsidiary company.

The same situation would apply when an award has been completed and work is taking place.

9 Challenges to surveyors' decisions

9.1 Introduction

The Act provides two routes by which surveyors' decisions can be challenged. The first is by involving the third surveyor, at the pre-award stage. The second is by appealing to the county court against an award, under s. 10(17).

It may also be possible to challenge an award indirectly, if the Act's procedures have not been properly followed or if the award goes beyond the powers given to surveyors by the Act (see part 6). A party who believes that an award is invalid may seek to establish this in court by seeking a declaration.

9.2 Role of the third surveyor

9.2.1 Nature of the role

A party-appointed surveyor who considers that his or her opposite number is taking an unreasonable attitude has the option of requesting the third surveyor's involvement to settle the point in dispute. The Act also allows the appointing owners the same right, although in practice it is fairly rare for an owner to take the initiative personally.

The third surveyor's decision will then be embodied in an award which will deal only with the dispute referred to him or her. The party-appointed surveyors will retain jurisdiction over all other matters referred to in the original notice.

9.2.2 Preliminary notification

Where party-appointed surveyors propose to refer a dispute to the third surveyor they should inform their appointing owner of the points at issue, the efforts they have made to reach agreement, and the impact in terms of time and cost of referring the dispute to the third surveyor. The owner may, for example, be prepared to concede the point in dispute rather than risk further delay and expense.

It is also advisable, before party-appointed surveyors refer a dispute to the third surveyor, to confirm in writing to their opposite number their intention to do so. Although the Act does not require this, it is suggested that failure to do so could be a matter taken into account in awarding costs.

9.2.3 Referral to third surveyor

The Act does not lay down the form of referral to the third surveyor. It is suggested, however, that, except in the most urgent cases, submissions should be in writing. They should clearly define the disputes on which the third surveyor's decision is sought, and attach all relevant documents.

They should be presented in such a way as to enable the third surveyor to form a clear idea of the points on which he or she is asked to decide, and the main areas of factual or technical dispute. This will avoid uncertainty as to the scope of the third surveyor's jurisdiction and to ensure that costs and time required by the referral are minimized.

It should also be made clear that the submissions are a formal request to the third surveyor to deal with the matter, not simply a request for guidance.

9.2.4 Procedure on referral to third surveyor

Once a dispute is referred to the third surveyor, the Act simply requires that he or she shall make the necessary award. The Act is silent as to both the procedure to be followed, and who is to control or decide the procedure. However, the words of the Act suggest an intention that the procedure is to be laid down by the third surveyor, who has responsibility to determine the disputed matters.

The Act does not specifically require the third surveyor to observe the rules of natural justice. However, the third surveyor's position is likely to be analogous to that of an adjudicator under Part II of the Housing Grants Construction and Regeneration Act 1996. It is now clear that such adjudicators are obliged to observe the rules of natural justice (*Discain Project Services Ltd* v *Opecprime Development Ltd.* [2000] BLR 402; *Woods Hardwick Ltd* v *Chiltern Air Conditioning* [2001] CILL 1698). It is, therefore, suggested that a third surveyor is similarly obliged. It therefore follows that:

- The third surveyor should give each party a fair opportunity to present its case and challenge the other party's case.
- The third surveyor should avoid, if possible, receiving information or submissions from one party in the absence of the other. Where he or she does receive information or submissions from one party in this way, a note should be made and sent to both parties.

Subject to this, the third surveyor is free to adopt whatever procedure appears appropriate. Where the dispute has been referred to him or her by way of written submissions from one surveyor, or owner, the third surveyor ought to call on the other surveyor or owner to reply to those submissions within a certain time. The third surveyor may well wish to visit the site, meet the parties' surveyors, and consider reports, drawings, photographs and other relevant material before reaching his or her decision.

9.2.5 Third surveyor's award

The third surveyor can only deal with the matters in dispute which are referred to him or her. The third surveyor does not, therefore, have power to carry out a general review of the previous actions of the party-appointed surveyors, still less to reopen any awards they have made.

The third surveyor is not required to give reasons for his or her award which, like any determination by surveyors under the Act, is more in the nature of an expert determination (*Chartered Society of Physiotherapy* v *Simmonds Church Smiles* [1995] 1 EGLR 155).

The award should deal with the costs incurred, pursuant to s. 10(13). Those costs are within the discretion of the third surveyor. The general practice in relation to awards by party-appointed surveyors is that the building owner will be required to pay the costs of the adjoining owner. It may be legitimate to depart from the general practice where the third surveyor considers that one party or his or her surveyor has behaved unreasonably. This may also be appropriate where the time and expense of the proceedings have been extended by one or both surveyors or owners raising matters of dispute out of proportion to the value and importance of the subject matter.

Section 10(15) of the Act deals with service of a third surveyor's award. The third surveyor is to serve it forthwith on the parties or their appointed surveyors after payment of his or her costs. The third surveyor is entitled to retain the award unless and until those costs are paid. In practice, he or she may prefer to serve the award on the party-appointed surveyors, and (though this is not mandatory) include in his or her award a provision that they shall forthwith serve the award on the parties.

9.3 Appeals to the county court

Section 10(17) of the Act confers a right of appeal by either party (i.e. building owner or adjoining owner) against an award. The appeal is to the county court and must be made within 14 days beginning with the day on which an award made under s. 10 is served on that party.

The 14-day time limit cannot be extended by the court or by agreement. However, if the last day for making the appeal occurs on a date when the court office is closed, the appeal can be made on the first day thereafter when the office is open.

An appeal is made by claim under Part 8 of the Civil Procedure Rules 1998 (CPR), which apply in the high court and county court. There is a prescribed claim form (Form N208). The claim should set out the grounds of appeal, and any written evidence intended to be relied upon should be attached. Form N208A includes guidance on completion of the claim form, and subsequent procedure.

The Act does not specify the grounds on which an appeal against an award can be made. However, in *Chartered Society of Physiotherapy* v *Simmonds Church Smiles* [1995] 1 EGLR 155 it was held that the court had complete power to review the award, and hear further evidence.

An appeal lies from the decision of the county court, with permission, to the court of appeal.

The procedure is regulated by Part 52 of the CPR.

9.4 Challenging the award

Section 10(16) of the Act provides that 'the award shall be conclusive and shall not except as provided by this section be questioned in any court'. This could be interpreted as precluding any challenge to the award except by way of appeal to the county court. However, it was decided by *Gyle-Thompson* v *Wall Street (Properties) Ltd* [1974] 1 All ER 295 that it is open to a party to contend that an award is *ultra vires*, and hence not a valid award, notwithstanding the absence of an appeal to the court. The distinction lies between a valid award, which can only be challenged by appeal, and an award which is invalid for failure to comply with the Act, which can be treated as invalid in subsequent proceedings. However, the invalidity of the award can also be raised on an appeal.

Appendix A: Precedents

Surveyor's Appointment and Authority

Party Wall etc. Act 1996

We hereby AUTHORIZE .... of .... to sign, issue, serve, receive and respond to all notices under the Party Wall etc. Act 1996 Act ('the Act') relating to the works currently proposed at [address].

In the event of a dispute arising within the meaning of the Act we hereby APPOINT the said .... as our surveyor in accordance with section 10 of the Act.

We further AUTHORIZE him/her to make all requests and appointments under the Act on our behalf which may be necessary to expedite the progress of the matter.

Dated the ...... day of .... 200[ ]

Signed:

Line of Junction Notice

Party Wall etc. Act 1996 section 1

To   (Adjoining owner)

of

*I/We   (Building owner)

of

as owner(s) of the land known as

which adjoins your land known as

HEREBY SERVE YOU WITH NOTICE THAT IN ACCORDANCE WITH *MY/OUR RIGHTS

*Under section 1(2), subject to your written consent
it is intended to build on the line of junction of the said lands a *party wall/party fence wall.
*Under section 1(5)
it is intended to build on the line of junction of the said lands a wall wholly on *my/our own land.
*Under section 1(6)
it is intended to place projecting footings and foundation on your land at *my/our expense.

Under section 7(4) it *is/is not proposed to employ special foundations, which would require your written consent.

The proposed works as shown on the accompanying drawings are:

It is intended to commence works *after one month/on the
or earlier by agreement.

In the event of matters arising for settlement *I/we would appoint as *my/our surveyor

of

Signed   (Date)
Authorized to sign   (Building owner)
On behalf of

*delete as appropriate

Acknowledgement of Line of Junction Notice

Party Wall etc. Act 1996 section 1(2)

To be completed and returned
to the building owner
or his/her surveyor

*I/We
of

having received the notice served

By
of

in respect of

which adjoins *my/our premises known as

and in relation to the works proposed under section 1(2) to build a party wall on the line of junction

*hereby consent to the above works
or
*hereby dissent from the above works and require that the wall be built wholly on your land

Signed   (Date)
*Authorized to sign   (Adjoining owner)
On behalf of

*delete as appropriate

Party Structure Notice

Party Wall etc. Act 1996 section 3

To   (Adjoining owner)

of

*I/We   (Building owner)

of

as owner(s) of

which adjoins your premises known as

HEREBY SERVE YOU WITH NOTICE THAT, IN ACCORDANCE WITH *MY/OUR RIGHTS:

Under section 2 (2), paragraphs
and with reference to the ***party structure/party fence wall** separating the above premises, it is intended to carry out the works detailed below after the expiration of **two months** from service of this notice.

The proposed works are:

It is intended to commence works *as soon as notice has run/on the
or earlier by agreement.

Under section 5, if you do not consent to the works within 14 days you are deemed to have dissented and a dispute is deemed to have arisen. In such case section 10 of the Act requires that both parties should concur in the appointment of a surveyor or should each appoint one surveyor and in those circumstances
*I/we would appoint

of

Signed   (Date)
Authorized to sign   (Building owner)
On behalf of

*delete as appropriate

Acknowledgement of Party Structure Notice

Party Wall etc. Act 1996 section 3

To be completed and returned
to the building owner
or his/her surveyor

*I/We

of

having received the notice served

By

of

in respect of

which adjoins *my/our premises known as

and in relation to the works proposed under section 2(2), paragraphs

*hereby consent to the above works

or

*hereby dissent from the above works and, a dispute having arisen, *concur in the appointment
of/appoint

of (address)

as *agreed/my surveyor

Signed
*Authorized to sign
On behalf of

(Date)
(Adjoining owner)

*delete as appropriate

Notice of Adjacent Excavation

Party Wall etc. Act 1996 section 6

To   (Adjoining owner)

of

*I/We   (Building owner)

of

as owners of

which adjoins your premises known as

HEREBY SERVE YOU WITH NOTICE THAT IN ACCORDANCE WITH *MY/OUR RIGHTS

Under section 6(1)
it is intended to build within 3 metres of your building and to a lower level than the bottom of your foundations, by carrying out the works detailed below, after the expiration of one month from the service of this notice.
or
*Under section 6(2)
it is intended to build within 6 metres of your building and to a depth as defined in the Act, by carrying out the works detailed below, after the expiration of one month from the service of this notice.

IT *IS/IS NOT PROPOSED TO UNDERPIN OR OTHERWISE STRENGTHEN OR SAFEGUARD THE FOUNDATIONS OF YOUR *BUILDING/STRUCTURE.

The accompanying plans and sections show the site and the excavation depth proposed.

The intended works are:

It is intended to commence works *as soon as notice has run/on the
or earlier by agreement.

Under section 6(7), if you do not consent to the works within 14 days you are deemed to have dissented and a dispute is deemed to have arisen. In such case section 10 of the Act requires that both parties should concur in the appointment of a surveyor or should each appoint one surveyor and in those circumstances
*I/we would appoint

of

Signed   (Date)
*Authorized to sign   (Building owner)
On behalf of

*delete as appropriate

Acknowledgement of Notice of Adjacent Excavation

Party Wall etc. Act 1996 section 6

To be completed and returned
to the building owner
or his/her surveyor

*I/We
of

having received the notice served

By
of

in respect of

which adjoins *my/our premises known as

*consent to your proposals
or
*dispute the necessity for underpinning or strengthening the foundations of *my/our building
or
*require you to underpin or strengthen the foundations of *my/our building

and a dispute having arisen, *concur in the appointment of/appoint Mr/Ms

of (address)

as *agreed/my surveyor.

Signed   (Date)
*Authorized to sign   (Adjoining owner)
On behalf of

*delete as appropriate

AN AWARD under the provisions of the Party Wall etc. Act 1996 to be
served on the appointing owners under section 10(14) thereof

WHEREAS .... of .... (hereinafter called 'the building owner') is an owner within the meaning of the Party Wall etc. Act 1996 (hereinafter referred to as 'the Act') of the premises known as .... (hereinafter called 'the building owner's property').

AND WHEREAS .... of .... (hereinafter called 'the adjoining owner') is an owner within the meaning of the Act of the premises known as .... (hereinafter called 'the adjoining owner's property').

AND WHEREAS on the .... day of .... 200[ ] the building owner served notice(s) on the adjoining owner under [section 1 and section 2 and section 3] of the Act of its intention to execute the building works described therein at or adjacent to the boundary between the building owner's property and the adjoining owner's property (hereinafter together called 'the two properties').

AND WHEREAS a dispute has arisen between the building owner and the adjoining owner (hereinafter together called 'the parties') within the meaning of the Act.

AND WHEREAS the building owner has appointed .... of .... (hereinafter called 'the building owner's surveyor') to act as its surveyor and the adjoining owner has appointed .... of .... (hereinafter called 'the adjoining owner's surveyor') to act as its surveyor.

AND WHEREAS the building owner's surveyor and the adjoining owner's surveyor (hereinafter together called 'the two surveyors') have selected .... of .... to act as third surveyor in accordance with the provisions of the Act. In the event of the third surveyor being unable or unwilling to act and their being unable jointly to agree upon a substitute, they have agreed that another third surveyor shall be appointed by the appointing officer of the relevant local authority in accordance with section 10(8) of the above Act.

NOW WE, the two surveyors, having inspected the two properties, DO HEREBY AWARD AND DETERMINE as follows:

1.   *(a)   That the wall separating the two properties is a party wall within the meaning of the Act.

     *(a)   That .... is an independent building standing close to or adjoining the building owner's property, within the meaning of the Act.

     (b)   That the said *wall/building as described in the attached schedule of condition is sufficient for the present purposes of the adjoining owner.

*delete as appropriate

(c) That the schedule of condition dated .... signed by and held on the files of the two surveyors and attached hereto forms part of this award.

(d) That the drawings numbered .... signed by and held on the files of the two surveyors and attached hereto form part of this award.

2. That after the delivery of the signed award the building owner shall be at liberty if it so chooses, but shall be under no obligation, to carry out the following works (hereinafter referred to as 'the works'):

(a)

(b)

(c)

3. That no material deviation from the works shall be made without the prior written agreement of the parties, or of the two surveyors acting on their behalf and with their express authority.

4. That if the building owner carries out the works it shall:

(a) Execute the whole of the works at the sole cost of the building owner.

(b) Take all reasonable precautions and provide all necessary support to retain the land and buildings comprised within the adjoining owner's property.

(c) Provide temporary weathering in the form of heavy duty felt and battens to those parts of the adjoining owner's property exposed as a result of the works and maintain this until permanent weathering has been provided unless otherwise agreed by the two surveyors.

(d) Make good all structural or decorative damage to the adjoining owner's property occasioned by the works in materials to match the existing fabric and finishes, to the reasonable satisfaction of the two surveyors, such making good to be executed upon completion of the works, or at any earlier time deemed appropriate by the two surveyors. If so required by the adjoining owner, make payment in lieu of carrying out the work to make the damage good, such sum to be determined by the two surveyors.

(e) Indemnify the adjoining owner in respect of injury to or loss of life of any person or damage to property caused by, or in consequence of, the execution of the works and the costs of making any justified claims. The building owner is to maintain or cause contractor(s) to maintain adequate insurance against such risks and provide evidence of this upon demand by the adjoining owner's surveyor.

(f) Permit the adjoining owner's surveyor to have access to the building owner's property at all reasonable times during the progress of the works.

(g) Carry out the whole of the works so far as practicable from the building owner's side of the boundary between the two properties. Where access to the adjoining owner's property is required, reasonable notice shall be given in accordance with section 8 of the

Act. That in the event of the building owner wishing to carry out the works from or to erect scaffolding on or over the adjoining owner's property for the purpose of the works, details thereof shall first be submitted to and approved by the two surveyors and such approval shall be subject to such conditions as the two surveyors may agree.

(h)   Remove any scaffolding or screens as soon as possible and clear away any dust and debris from time to time as necessary, or when agreed by the two surveyors.

(i)   Provide the two surveyors with such method statements as they may reasonably require in relation to the works that are the subject of this award prior to carrying out the works.

5.   That the building owner, its professional advisers and contractors, may enter upon the adjoining owner's property for the purpose of checking constructional details thereof to facilitate the design and execution of the works, insofar as such access is reasonably necessary and reasonable notice is given in accordance with the Act.

6.   That the building owner's surveyor shall be permitted access to the adjoining owner's property from time to time during the progress of the works at reasonable times and after giving reasonable notice.

7.   That the whole of the works shall be executed in accordance with the Building Regulations, and all requirements and by-laws of statutory authorities where these apply and shall be executed in a proper and workman-like manner in sound and suitable materials in accordance with the terms of this award to the reasonable satisfaction of the two surveyors.

8.   That the works shall be carried through with reasonable expedition after commencement and so as to avoid unnecessary inconvenience to the adjoining owner or occupiers.

9.   That the signed awards shall be delivered forthwith to the parties. An unsigned copy thereof shall be provided for the adjoining owner's surveyor. A further copy shall be provided for the building owner's contractor who shall be made aware of its contents.

10.   That the building owner shall provide to the adjoining owner a set of the 'as built' drawings upon completion of the works, at the sole cost of the building owner.

11.   That the building owner shall immediately on the signing of this award pay the adjoining owner's surveyor's fees of £............... plus VAT in connection with the preparation of this award, and .... subsequent inspection(s) of the works. In the event of damage being caused or other contingencies or variations arising, a further fee shall be payable at a rate of £............ per hour plus VAT.

12.   That the said surveyors reserve the right to make and issue any further award or awards that may be necessary, as provided in the Act.

13.   That this award shall be null and void if the permitted works are not commenced within 12 months from the date hereof.

14.   That this award is made without prejudice to the rights of any other persons or bodies having an interest in the said party wall.

15. That nothing in this award shall be held as conferring, admitting or affecting any right to light or air or any other easement whatsoever.

IN WITNESS WHEREOF we have set our hands this   day of
Two Thousand and

....
Surveyor to the building owner   Surveyor to the adjoining owner
WITNESS   WITNESS
Name: ....   Name:..
Address: ....   Address: ....
....
Occupation: ....   Occupation:................................

Draft Letters

1. DRAFT LETTER TO ACCOMPANY A TYPICAL SECTION 3 OR 6 NOTICE TO ADJOINING OWNER

Dear ....

(ADDRESS)

Under the Party Wall etc. Act 1996 our clients .... are obliged to serve you with the accompanying notice of their intention to carry out works likely to affect your premises.

This letter is to explain in less formal terms that if you disagree with any of the proposed works you should appoint your own surveyor to safeguard your interests. As the works proposed are minor you may feel that you can concur in the appointment of .... as agreed surveyor, who will impartially regulate matters affecting us both. The surveyor's fee, under all normal circumstances, will be paid by my clients. Naturally my clients will also be responsible for making good any damage that their works may cause.

I would be grateful to learn whether or not you agree to the works proposed and, if you are intending to appoint your own surveyor, if you would let me know who this will be. Please complete and return the enclosed acknowledgement form giving this information and kindly tell me of any other person having an interest in the property, either as landlord or tenant.

I would be pleased to explain in further detail the formalities involved in these matters if you so wish.

Yours .... *(Signature)*

Note

Notices will normally be sent to a lay adjoining owner and this accompanying letter will assist in giving meaning to the legal requirements.

2. DRAFT LETTER REQUIRING AN ADJOINING OWNER TO APPOINT A SURVEYOR

Dear ....

(ADDRESS)

Party Wall etc. Act 1996

On (date) notice was served upon you concerning proposed works affecting your property. As you were advised at that time, the above Act required you to appoint a surveyor if you dissent from the proposals. You have not signified your assent within 14 days and therefore you are deemed to have dissented and must now appoint a surveyor.

As the building owner's surveyor, I formally call upon you to appoint a surveyor in accordance with section 10 of the above Act, or to concur in the appointment of ...., and if you fail to do so within ten days, as required by that section, the building owner will make an appointment on your behalf.

Yours .... *(Signature)*

Note

Under section 10(4) the adjoining owner is obliged to appoint his or her surveyor within ten days of a written request where a difference has arisen. This letter provides such a formal notice.

3. DRAFT LETTER REQUIRING ANY ONE OF THE THREE SURVEYORS TO ACT

Dear ....

(ADDRESS)

Party Wall etc. Act 1996

On (date) I sent you a draft award for your consideration but have received no reply.

In accordance with section 10(6) and (7) of the above Act, I now formally call upon you to act effectively and give you notice that if you fail to do so within ten days, I will exercise my authority to proceed *ex parte*.

Yours .... *(Signature)*

Note

This gives ten days' written notice, in accordance with section 10(6) and (7), to any of the three surveyors to act. Failure to do so will enable the other party to proceed *ex parte*.

4. DRAFT LETTER TO THE APPOINTING OWNERS TO ACCOMPANY THE PARTY WALL AWARD

Dear ....

(ADDRESS)

Party Wall etc. Act 1996

I enclose the party wall award made and signed by the two appointed surveyors which sets out the rights and duties in connection with the proposed work.

I must point out that, under the Act, section 10(17), you are legally entitled to appeal within 14 days against the award in the county court if you feel that it has been made improperly. To the best of my knowledge, however, there is nothing in the award which should cause you to take this action.

Yours .... *(Signature)*

Note

You must send the award and you should inform the appointing owner that he or she has the right of appeal, although it is unlikely that he or she will wish to exercise it. The Act obliges the surveyors to deliver the award to their appointing owners promptly and this letter, when accompanying the award, sets out the legal position without encouraging the owners to appeal.

Appendix B: Specimen Schedule of Condition

The schedule of condition records the condition of relevant parts of an adjoining owner's property before the start of the building owner's works. It enables the surveyors, at a later date, to determine the extent of the building owner's liability for damage caused by the works.

It should be as detailed as necessary for its purpose but should not extend to areas which are too remote to be damaged, nor include irrelevant descriptions. It should, for example, include all signs of cracking and damp damage within 1–2m of the works, or the whole of the room adjacent to the party wall and within a greater distance if the case warrants it. Often the simple description of an area of surface plaster crazing will be more useful than a detailed description of every hair crack forming it. However, it should generally not include matters such as paint colours and descriptions of door furniture.

It is common for it to be written in the 'Area, Description, Condition' format, and to begin on the top floor. Photographs are sometimes used. However, these can be time consuming and costly in reproduction. Furthermore, although capable of showing a general state of dilapidation, they generally provide little assistance in determining whether, for example, a hair crack has worsened. Sketches may also be useful in identifying areas of damage or patterns of cracking.

The cover sheet will state that it is a schedule of condition of those parts of the property in question (identified by its address) close or adjacent to the site (again identified by its address). It will give the date on which the schedule was taken and may include reference to the name(s) of the appointed surveyor(s).

It will then adopt a format similar to that in the following example.

SCHEDULE OF CONDITION

OF

6 GREEN MEWS

Taken on: 16 July 2002

Preliminary Notes

1. This schedule of condition was prepared by Joe Bloggs of Trusty Surveyors and John Smith of Professional Surveyors on 16 July 2002.

2. It was prepared in connection with an award for works at 7 Green Mews to be carried out pursuant to the Party Wall etc. Act 1996.

3. For the purpose of the schedule the front elevation of the property is deemed to face due south and all other directions are given accordingly.

Item	Description	Condition
EXTERNAL		
FRONT ELEVATION		
Walls	Elevation constructed in brick work, decorated with masonry paint. Rendered parapet at high level with lead cappings. Timber bresummer at head of ground floor windows and doors, painted.	Some unevenness to render at high level parapet beneath paint finish. One split in paint adjacent to party wall line at high level. Otherwise, paint all intact and clean.
Joinery	Timber windows and garage doors and front door decorated with gloss paint.	Paint in slightly weathered condition with flaking paint to bottom rails of windows. All glazing intact. Paint generally flaking to base of garage doors and some flaking paint to dark painted plinth at base of wall.
Rear roof slope (as viewed from adjoining property)	Pitched roof clad in Welsh slates. Lead flashings to brick parapet.	On half of roof slope closer to No. 7 party wall two slopes have chipped corners and one has slipped. Flashing on party wall curled on bottom edge and not dressed flat to slates.
INTERNAL		
1st FLOOR		
REAR KITCHEN		
Ceiling	Plasterboard ceiling decorated with emulsion paint.	Ceiling slopes down to west.

Walls	Plastered walls decorated with emulsion paint. Tiled splashback around kitchen units. Fitted floor units on north and east walls and fitted wall units on party wall.	Open joint at junction of west wall and ceiling continues down north-west corner and through tile grout to top of cable penetrating behind tiles. Crack hairline. Fine hairline crack in south-west corner runs down from ceiling to level with head of door.
		In south-east corner, hairline crack, partially staggered at high level, runs down from ceiling to behind microwave on shelf bracket. Adjacent to this, horizontal hairline crack to underside of projecting timber joist runs from south-east corner over top of cupboards where it disappears from view.
Floor	Timber floor laid with laminate flooring.	Floor slopes down towards south-west with creaky floor-boards in centre but floor otherwise sound and laminate flooring tight jointed.
Window	Timber casement window decorated with gloss paint.	Left casement operates correctly, right casement catches when opening. All glazing intact.
		Fine open joint to junction of window sill and window frame extending from left side of sill to just beyond left casement.
Door	Timber fully glazed door decorated with gloss paint.	Door slightly warped protruding into room at foot preventing closing home.

Front Bedroom

Ceiling	Lath and plaster ceiling decorated with emulsion paint.	Ceiling generally uneven and slightly bowed. Bowing particularly noticeable sloping down from front elevation.
		Hairline crack over head of left window runs into ceiling for one metre. Where crack terminates, evidence of patch repair in plaster. 500mm to west of this is one popped nail head.

Evidence of previous crack extending from the one that extends from the window that previously ran to the north wall since filled and decorated. Areas of unevenness on line approx. 500mm from north wall and one re-opened split 10mm long.

Open hairline joints in cornice in corners of room and over door to adjoining bedroom on west side.

Walls	Plastered walls decorated with wallpaper.	No defects identified.
Floor	Timber floor laid with fitted carpet.	Floor slopes down to north. Otherwise floor sound.
Windows	Timber double hung sliding sash window and pair of French doors, all decorated with gloss paint.	Window operates correctly. Paint flaking to bottom rail of lower sash and paint flaking to top surface of external sills. All glazing intact.
Door	Timber flush door decorated with gloss paint.	Door very slightly warped protruding into room at foot preventing latch closing home.

Appendix C: Further Reading

Anstey, J. (1998) *Party Walls and What to do With Them* (Fifth Edition), RICS Books

Anstey, J. & North, G. (2000) *A Practical Manual for Party Wall Surveyors*, RICS Books

Anstey, J. & Vegoda, V. (1997) *An Introduction to the Party Wall etc. Act 1996*, Lark Productions

Bickford-Smith, S. & Sydenham, C. (1997) *Party Walls: The New Law*, Jordans

Chynoweth, P. (2001) *The Party Wall etc. Act 1996: Defining the Role of the Appointed Surveyor*, RICS Foundation Research Paper, Volume 4, Number 2

Morrow, N. S. (1998) *Party Walls Workbook*, RIBA Publications

Pyramus & Thisbe Club (1996) *The Party Wall Act Explained: A Commentary on the Party Wall etc. Act 1996* (The Green Book), Parrot House Press

Useful websites

Pyramus & Thisbe Club: www.partywalls.org.uk

Party Wall Discussion Forum: www.partywallforum.co.uk

Party Wall Case Summaries: www.partywalls.com

RICS Boundaries & Party Walls Working Group: www.rics.org.uk